Junior Martial Arts
Hand-Eye Coordination

Junior Martial Arts

ALL AROUND GOOD HABITS
CONFIDENCE
CONCENTRATION
HAND-EYE COORDINATION
HANDLING PEER PRESSURE
SAFETY
SELF-DEFENSE
SELF-DISCIPLINE
SELF-ESTEEM

JUNIOR MARTIAL ARTS
Hand-Eye Coordination

KIM ETINGOFF

MASON CREST

Mason Crest
450 Parkway Drive, Suite D
Broomall, PA 19008
www.masoncrest.com

Printed and bound in the United States of America.

First printing
9 8 7 6 5 4 3 2 1

Series ISBN: 978-1-4222-2731-2
ISBN: 978-1-4222-2735-0
ebook ISBN: 978-1-4222-9068-2

The Library of Congress has cataloged the
        hardcopy format(s) as follows:

        Library of Congress Cataloging-in-Publication Data

Etingoff, Kim.
  Hand-eye coordination / Kim Etingoff.
      pages cm. – (Junior martial arts)
  ISBN 978-1-4222-2735-0 (hardcover) – ISBN 978-1-4222-2731-2 (series) – ISBN 978-1-4222-9068-2
(ebook)
  1. Martial arts–Juvenile literature. 2. Eye-hand coordination–Juvenile literature. I. Title.
  GV1101.35.E788 2014
  796.8–dc23
                                            2013004747

Contents

MORE THAN FIGHTING

Have you ever watched a martial arts movie? Were martial artists jumping across the screen and fighting ten bad guys at once?

Movies can make martial arts seem almost like magic. And they have made lots of kids (and adults) excited about taking martial arts classes.

Once you start taking martial arts, though, you learn they're not magic. But they are still really cool. You learn how to move your body in different ways. You learn how to feel good about yourself.

So, even if real-life martial arts aren't quite like the movies, they're fun and good for you. You have to spend a lot of time and energy to get really good. But all that work is worth it. Martial arts can make you a better person.

Martial Arts, Explained

Martial arts are all forms of **self-defense**. Each kind of martial art teaches you different things. But most martial arts teach you how to keep yourself safe from someone trying to hurt you. That doesn't mean martial arts are all about fighting. Most martial arts are about learning that you don't have to fight. They're about making your body and mind stronger.

The idea of martial arts is very old. The first forms of martial arts started around thousands of years ago. In the past, they were used for protection. Many of them used real weapons. They were also used to teach students how to become better people.

Today, we mostly use martial arts as a way to have fun and become stronger. Most people don't really use them in real fights. There are plenty of other reasons to take martial arts or become a martial arts master.

Students of all ages learn martial arts in classes. The teacher is called a master or sensei. The teacher is in charge of making sure all his or her students learn and get better. Teachers have spent a long time learning martial arts.

There are all kinds of martial arts. Each one looks a little different. Some are practiced alone, and some with partners. Some use more hands and some use more feet. Some use fake weapons.

Different martial arts come from different places in the world. Many of the martial arts you might have heard about first started in Asia.

Karate is one of the most famous martial arts. It's from Japan. Kung fu (or wushu) is a bunch of Chinese martial arts. Taekwondo comes from Korea.

There are also martial arts from other parts of the world. Capoeira and Brazilian jiu-jitsu are from Brazil in South America. Fencing, boxing, and wrestling were created in Europe.

You can take classes for any of those martial arts. And there are lots more out there. You might take a class in one martial art and decide it's not for you. There are lots more to try, so you can keep searching.

Capoeira Moves

Capoeira is a little different from a lot of other martial arts. Everyone in the room stands in a circle. Two people are in the middle. They are the ones who are going to play the capoeira game. People on the outside of the circle might be singing or playing music. A lot of capoeira has to do with learning how to avoid getting hit. The basic move in capoeira is called ginga. You never stand still in capoeira. Instead, you do the ginga movement. You move back and forth with your feet. It helps keep you away from an attack. It also helps you surprise the other student and make moves she wasn't expecting.

Body and Mind

There's a lot going on when you practice martial arts. First, there are lots of moves to do with your body. That's what you see when you watch someone practicing martial arts.

Martial arts are full of kicks and punches. There are blocks and throws. In some kinds of martial arts, like karate, you break wooden boards in half with your hands.

Martial arts can be good exercise because you move around a lot. You get stronger. You get more **flexible**. Your **balance** gets better. Martial arts help your body in lots of ways.

There's also a lot going on in your mind when you do martial arts. Martial arts teach you more than just how to move. They teach you new ways of thinking. You learn how to focus and concentrate. You learn how to respect your teacher and other students. You learn to be more confident in what you can do.

All this takes a lot of time. You can't go to one martial arts class and learn everything all at once. Martial arts take practice. So does learning how to concentrate and building confidence. But if you stick with it, you'll see what martial arts can do for you!

Everyday Skills

Martial arts can help you outside of karate or taekwondo class. Learning from martial arts can help you every day, in school, at home, and with friends. Martial arts teach you life **skills**. Life skills are abilities you can use in school, at home, and with friends.

Maybe you're not so good at focusing in school. You can't seem to pay attention to the teacher. You get bored reading. You never do your homework because you don't have enough patience.

Martial arts can help you learn to focus. When you're practicing a martial art, you're concentrating really hard on getting better. You watch the teacher closely. You think hard about what your body is doing. You practice a lot to get a move right. That's all teaching you how to concentrate.

After practicing martial arts, you might find it's easier to focus in school. Maybe you can sit still while the teacher is talking. You might have more patience or be able to read longer. You might find you can finish your homework before going to play. School may get a little easier!

It's not just school that could get better. You can learn to get along with your friends and family better, too.

In martial arts class, you learn respect. That means paying attention to other people's feelings. Your teacher will ask that you respect him in class. You'll also learn to respect other students and yourself.

If you learn to respect other people, your friends and family will thank you! You won't get in as many fights if you know how to think about other people. You might think twice before taking your brother's toys. You won't call your classmates names.

Hand-Eye Coordination

One of the things martial arts teach you is hand-eye coordination. Hand-eye coordination is how well your eyes and hands work together.

There's a lot going on in your brain when your hands and eyes work together. First, your eyes see something, like a ball coming toward you. They send a mes-

sage about seeing the ball to your brain. Then your brain tells your hands to move. They catch the ball.

When we're babies, our hand-eye coordination isn't very good. It gets better as we get older. Some people have better hand-eye coordination than others.

But unless we have a disease, we all have enough hand-eye coordination to live our lives. We use hand-eye coordination every day.

We use it to get dressed. We use it to make breakfast and eat. We use it to get on the bus—and to write, read, and play with friends at school. Any time you're using your hands, you use hand-eye coordination. Think of all the things you do with your hands every day.

Hand-eye coordination is also a part of martial arts. And the more you practice martial arts, the better your hand-eye coordination will be!

A Hand-Eye Coordination Test

If you want to see how good your own hand-eye coordination is, do a test. You need a tennis ball, a wall, and a stopwatch. Stand about six feet (or two meters) from the wall. You're going to be throwing the ball underarm against the wall with one hand. Then you'll catch the ball with your other hand. So, if you decide to throw the ball with your left hand, catch it with your right hand. You want to see how many times you can do this in 30 seconds. Set your stopwatch and go!

If you can throw and catch the ball more than 35 times, you have really good hand-eye coordination. Most people can do it between 20 and 30 times. Your hand-eye coordination isn't that great if it's less than 15 times. The younger you are, the fewer times you'll probably be able to catch the ball. That's normal. Even if you're not happy with the results, you can always practice and get better!

HAND-EYE COORDINATION & MARTIAL ARTS

2

Martial arts teach you lots of things. They make you a better person in many ways. Learning martial arts helps you think about things in new ways. It will help your body get stronger. Part of that is getting better at hand-eye coordination.

Defense

Think about what you have to do when you're practicing martial arts. You have to defend yourself! And defending yourself means keeping away from another student's fists and feet.

Many martial arts students practice punching mitts like these. Using these kinds of mitts, students can practice getting their hand-eye coordination.

 **14** HAND-EYE COORDINATION

You have to be able to see where the other person is going to punch or kick you. And then you want to block it. Or move away from it.

The only way you can do that is if you have good hand-eye coordination. First, your eyes have to see what's going to happen. Even that can be hard. Your **opponent** might be moving really fast. And there's a lot going on. It can be hard to even know where to look or to see what's going to hit you.

Your eyes have to send that message to your brain. Then your brain decides what to do. Your brain sends a message back to your hands and feet.

Maybe your brain decides to go for an arm-block to keep you from getting hit. If you have good hand-eye coordination, you can get your hand and arm up in time. If you don't, you'll feel the punch.

A lot of things could go wrong. Your eyes might not have seen the punch coming. Or your brain might not be able to decide what to do fast enough. Or your hand and arm didn't get into place fast enough.

Any of these things could happen. When you first start martial arts, they probably will—a lot!

But with practice, your hand-eye coordination gets better. You know what part of your opponent's body to focus on. Your eyes know where to look. They'll see the punch coming.

After practice, your brain knows what to decide. At first, you won't know the moves very well. But then you'll learn proper arm-blocking moves. You'll practice them over and over again. And your brain will remember them. It will make a quick choice to use the right arm-block.

And your hand and arm will know what to do. Once they get the message from your brain, you'll move them up in time. They'll be in the right place to block the punch.

Punching and Kicking

Some martial arts are more about blocking punches and kicks or getting out of the way. In others, you have to learn to attack. In taekwondo, students focus on learning kicks. In akido, students don't use as many punches and kicks. Akdio students learn to throw people or keep them from moving.

Students of these martial arts practice fighting together. They may punch and kick each other. But they aren't trying to hurt each other. You're not meant to hurt people with the things you learn in martial arts class. Practice fighting is called **sparring**.

Just like you got punched in the last example, you might have to punch someone else. That involves hand-eye coordination too.

You have to know where to place your punch. And you have to know when to do it. Again, your eyes see where you want to put your fist. They tell your brain. Then your brain decides how to punch and tells your hand where to go.

This also takes practice. You probably won't get it right the first few times you do it.

The more you practice, the faster and better you'll be. But don't worry if it takes awhile. Hand-eye coordination can take a long time to learn.

What Else?

Martial arts help your body in other ways besides hand-eye coordination. You get better at balancing. You'll have to balance on one foot sometimes. You have to keep your balance when jumping and kicking. You'll also become more flexible. Your teacher might have you do stretches before class. And during class, you'll be using your muscles in new ways. That will help make them looser and more flexible. You might get stronger too, or lose weight if you need to. Martial arts are good for your body in lots of ways!

Back and Forth

Taking martial arts will help you improve your hand-eye coordination. But it works the other way too. Hand-eye coordination will help you get better at martial arts.

Sparring is a big part of learning martial arts. Practicing fighting with a partner is a great way to test how well you know your martial art. Sparring also tests your hand-eye coordination.

When you start practicing martial arts, you'll get a lot better at things like hand-eye coordination. By the time you get to harder levels, you'll have some hand-eye coordination to help you out.

Higher levels have more difficult moves. You might have to do harder things with your hands. You have to move faster.

Of course, you'll always be improving your hand-eye coordination. No one has perfect hand-eye coordination. Even if you're in higher martial arts levels, you can still get better!

Eskrima

Eskrima is a kind of martial art from the Philippines. It uses sticks and other weapons. It's a good martial art to help you get better at hand-eye coordination. You learn how to use the sticks, which are controlled by your hands. You pay a lot more attention to what your hands are doing when they're holding weapons! With practice, you can use the sticks to keep opponents with other sticks away from you. You can also be successful at attacking an opponent with your sticks.

GETTING BETTER AT HAND-EYE COORDINATION

Martial arts offer a way to improve your hand-eye coordination. But you don't have to only practice hand-eye coordination in the martial arts studio. You can practice it all the time!

Sports

Sports stars usually have great hand-eye coordination. They have to be able to hit, catch, and throw balls. The more you practice sports, the more you're practicing hand-eye coordination.

Some sports use more hand-eye coordination than others. Soccer, for example, doesn't use as much as other sports. It does let you practice coordination, though.

Racquet sports are some of the best. Racquet sports include tennis, squash, badminton, and even ping-pong.

You have to use a lot of hand-eye coordination in these sports. That's how you play the game! You have to be able to see where the ball is coming toward you. Then you have to be able to hit the ball back to your opponent.

Try not to get frustrated if these sports are hard for you at first. The good thing about racquet sports is that you get a lot of chances to hit the ball in every game. Every time you hit the ball, or try to hit it, you're practicing hand-eye coordination.

Sports that use bats or sticks are also good for hand-eye coordination. Professional baseball and softball players, for example, have really great hand-eye coordination. They can see balls coming at them at over 90 miles per hour. And they can use their hands to swing the bat just right and hit the ball. They also throw and catch balls a lot.

It's not quite so hard when you're playing as a kid. You get plenty of chances to practice your hand-eye coordination throwing, catching, and swinging the bat. Other good hand-eye coordination sports using sticks include lacrosse, field hockey, and ice hockey.

Video Games

Video games and computer games can be fun. They're also a good hand-eye coordination workout.

Video games are all about hand-eye coordination. The action on the screen is moving fast. Lots of things are going on and you have to pay attention. You have to dodge attacks and attack opponents. You might have to solve a puzzle or go on an adventure.

Once your eyes see what you have to do, you still have to do it. Your brain is in charge of making choices about what to do on screen. Your hands are in charge of making your choices happen. Your hands are on the controller. They make your character on screen move in certain ways.

Video games are good because the only things you're concentrating on are what you see and how your hands are moving. You don't have to worry about how the rest of your body should move, like in sports. All you're doing is hand-eye coordination.

So, the next time you play a video or computer game, you can tell your parents that you're practicing your hand-eye coordination. Maybe they'll let you play longer!

Life-Saving Video Games

Even surgeons use video games to get better at hand-eye coordination. One study found that surgeons who played video games made fewer mistakes during surgery and performed surgery faster. They were able to practice hand-eye coordination. A doctor has to make tiny movements with her hands and fingers. She has to do everything right to help people stay healthy. In surgery, hand-eye coordination saves lives!

Playing video games can be a great way to learn better hand-eye coordination. When you play video games, your eyes, brain, and thumbs have to work together quickly. Those skills can help in the real world, too!

Getting Better at Hand-Eye Coordination

Arts and Crafts

There are even more things you can do to improve your hand-eye coordination. Making arts and crafts is one of them.

When you do art or make crafts, you use your hands a lot. You have to focus on what you're drawing or putting together. To make something you're proud of, you have to make the right movements with your hands.

You could color in a coloring book. Coloring in the lines takes hand-eye coordination. It's one of the first ways really little kids start to get better at hand-eye coordination.

You could try sewing or knitting. You could sculpt with clay or do pottery. You could draw or paint. You could make models of planes.

You have to be careful when you're working on arts and crafts. You want to get things just right. Cutting, pasting, drawing, and sewing all take hand-eye coordination.

Pretty much any art or craft you can think of uses hand-eye coordination. All arts and crafts make you control your hands. So let your imagination loose and make whatever you'd like while building better hand-eye coordination!

Practice in Martial Arts

Of course, you can practice hand-eye coordination during martial arts too. Just by doing martial arts, you'll get better at it.

But maybe you want to get even better at hand-eye coordination. You play a sport and want to practice hand-eye coordination more.

You can ask your martial arts teacher for activities that help your hand-eye coordination. Each type of martial art will have its own exercises for hand-eye coordination.

Your teacher might have you train with fake weapons. Or jump rope. Or try a new punching move that you haven't seen yet. Chances are, she'll have something to teach you.

Karate Juggling

Not all the exercises you do in karate are kicks, punches, and blocks. Your teacher will have you do all sorts of things to practice your balance and hand-eye coordination. Your karate teacher might even have you juggle! Juggling makes you focus really hard on hand-eye coordination. You have to see where the balls are in the air. Then you have to catch them over and over again. Once you get good at juggling, you can use those skills in karate itself. You'll aim your punches better!

HAND-EYE COORDINATION AND YOUR LIFE

Hand-eye coordination is a useful part of martial arts. It's also part of your everyday life. No matter where you live or what you like to do, you use hand-eye coordination all the time.

Think about a normal day. You start using hand-eye coordination right from the beginning. You get out of bed and get dressed. Putting on clothes takes **communication** between your eyes and hands.

During breakfast, bringing a spoon or a fork from your plate to your mouth takes hand-eye coordination. So does drinking from a glass.

It takes hand-eye coordination to pack up your school bag, open the door into school, and get a drink of water from the water fountain. The rest of your day is filled with hand-eye coordination too. It's hard to think of anything we do that doesn't use this skill!

In School

You use hand-eye coordination a lot in school. From the beginning of the day to the end, you have to use your eyes and hands together.

Writing is one of the best examples of hand-eye coordination. Writing is much easier when you can see what you're doing. If you know how a letter is supposed to look, you can make your hand write that letter.

When you're first learning writing, it's hard. That's because you don't know how the letters are supposed to look. Your hand isn't used to writing letters. As you practice, you learn the letters. And your hand-eye coordination gets much better.

Try writing with your eyes closed. You know the letters, and you've written them a lot. But it's really hard to write without seeing what you're doing. The letters are all wrong. And you probably didn't write in a straight line.

You need hand-eye coordination to type too, at least at first. When you're learning to type, you don't know where all the letters are yet. You have to look at the keyboard to tell your hands what to do.

Later on, you won't need your eyes as much. You might even be able to close your eyes and type at the same time. But it's really important to start learning how to type. Typing is one of the main ways to use a computer.

Hand-eye coordination is also important in gym. No matter what sport you're playing, you're using hand-eye coordination at least a little. Playing sports in gym can help you develop hand-eye coordination for the other parts of your life.

You use hand-eye coordination in other classes too. You need hand-eye coordination in art class, for example. If you get more hand-eye coordination through martial arts, you might become a better artist. You'll be better at telling your hands to do certain things.

If you have to draw a bunch of things in art class, you'll have an easier time with better hand-eye coordination. Your eyes notice all the lines and curves on the things you're drawing. Then your brain can tell your hand how to copy them down on paper. You probably never expected that practicing karate or jiu-jitsu would make you a better artist!

Clapping and running games can put your hand-eye coordination to the test. You might not even know it, but many games we play on the playground help to teach you better hand-eye coordination.

With Friends

When you're with friends, chances are you're using hand-eye coordination. Any time you play, you're using it.

Maybe you and your friends like to play board games. You move the pieces on the board around with your hands. But you can't just move them anywhere. You have to move them to the right spot. You see where you're supposed to move your piece with your eyes.

Or maybe your friends like to play on the playground after school. You use your hands a lot, to swing on the monkey bars and to climb up ladders. If you couldn't see, it would be hard to know where to put your hands. So you use your eyes to see and to tell your hands where to go.

You and your friends also like to explore outside. You lift up rocks to find bugs and worms. You make forts out of leaves or snow. You play tag out on the lawn or in the park. Just like everything else, all those activities use hand-eye coordination.

Problems

Almost all of us have enough hand-eye coordination to get through a normal day. Most of us just need to practice to get a little better. But some people have problems with hand-eye coordination. They are born without much hand-eye coordination. Some people have problems seeing. If you can't see, you can't let your brain know what's coming. And then your brain can't tell your hands what to do. Someone might not be able to tell if things are near or far away. Or they can't see things clearly. All of that could get in the way of hand-eye coordination. Other people have a problem moving. Their eyes are fine, but something goes wrong between the brain and the hands. With help, most people with hand-eye coordination problems can get better and have normal lives.

No matter what you're doing, you're probably using hand-eye coordination. Almost all of us know how to use at least some hand-eye coordination. But we can always get better at it.

Martial arts can help you improve your hand-eye coordination. The punches and kicks that you do in martial arts help your eyes, brain, and hands work together. And that will let you do lots of things better, from writing, to sports, to art!

Focus Mitts

If you want a little extra practice in your taekwondo or karate class, use focus mitts. Focus mitts are pads you wear on your hands. They're easy to see. They help you hit a target with your hands or feet. And they make your hand-eye coordination better. Another person can put them on too. Then you can practice a taekwondo side kick or a karate short punch.

Words to know

balance: Your ability to stand up straight, catch yourself when you fall, and stand on one leg.

communication: Sending a message between two people or things.

flexible: Able to bend or stretch the body.

opponent: Anyone you practice fighting against during martial arts class.

self-defense: Stopping another person from hurting you and making sure you're safe from danger.

skills: Things you learn that help you become a better person or live a better life.

sparring: Pretend fighting.

Find Out More

Online

All Star Activities
www.allstaractivities.com/sports/karate/Karate-belt-system.htm

KidzWorld: Martial Arts Quiz
www.kidzworld.com/quiz/5917-quiz-martial-arts-trivia

PBS Kids
pbskids.org/itsmylife/body/solosports/article2.html

In Books

Ancona, George. *Capoeira: Game! Dance! Martial Art!* Lee & Low Books, 2007.

Goodman, Didi. *The Kids' Karate Workbook: A Take-Home Training Guide for Young Martial Artists.* Berkeley, Cal.: Blue Snake Books, 2009.

Iedwab, Claudio. *The Peaceful Way: A Children's Guide to the Traditions of the Martial Arts.* Rochester, Ver.: Destiny Books, 2001.

Wiseman, Blaine. *Martial Arts.* New York: AV2 Books, 2010.

Index

About the Author

Kim Etingoff lives in Boston, Massachusetts, spending part of her time working on farms. Kim writes educational books for young people on topics including health, nutrition, and more.

Picture Credits